Why We Measure

by Janine Scott

Content and Reading Adviser: Mary Beth Fletcher, Ed.D.
Educational Consultant/Reading Specialist
The Carroll School, Lincoln, Massachusetts

Spyglass
BOOKS

COMPASS POINT BOOKS
Minneapolis, Minnesota

Compass Point Books
3109 West 50th Street, #115
Minneapolis, MN 55410

Visit Compass Point Books on the Internet at *www.compasspointbooks.com*
or e-mail your request to *custserv@compasspointbooks.com*

Photographs ©: Phil Bulgasch, cover, 4, 5, 10, 13, 14, 19; Ken Martin/Visuals Unlimited, 6 (left);
Comstock, 6 (right), 11; Index Stock Imagery/Lawrence Sawyer, 7; George Disario/Corbis, 8;
RubberBall Productions, 9; Richard Morrell/Corbis, 12; Photo Network/Myrleen Cate, 15 (left);
Photo Network/Esbin-Anderson, 15 (right); Bachmann/The Image Finders, 16; Eric Sanford/
Tom Stack & Associates, 17; Jim Baron/The Image Finders, 18.

Project Manager: Rebecca Weber McEwen
Editors: Heidi Schoof and Patricia Stockland
Photo Researcher: Svetlana Zhurkina
Designer: Jaime Martens
Illustrator: Anna-Maria Crum

Library of Congress Cataloging-in-Publication Data
Scott, Janine.
    Why we measure / by Janine Scott.
        p. cm. — (Spyglass books)
Summary: Uses real-life examples to demonstrate the importance of
measuring and measuring correctly.
Includes bibliographical references and index.
    ISBN 0-7565-0449-X (hardcover : alk. paper)
    1. Mensuration—Juvenile literature. [1. Measurement.] I. Title.
    II. Series.
    QA465 .S37 2003
    530.8—dc21   2002015745

Contents

When Things Go Wrong . . . 4

Too Tall 6

Splash! 8

Ouch! 10

Burned to a Crisp 12

Bubbles Everywhere 14

Ticket Time 16

The Right Tool 18

Fun Facts 20

Glossary 22

Learn More 23

Index 24

NOTE: Glossary words are in *bold* the first time they appear.

When Things Go Wrong

People need to *measure* things every day.
If people do not measure carefully, they can make a big mess!

Did You Know?

When you pick up your backpack, you are measuring to see if it is too heavy to carry.

Too Tall

People need to measure height carefully.

Truck drivers need to know how tall their trucks are so they don't get stuck in a tunnel.

Did You Know?

Carpenters like to say, "Measure *twice,* cut once." This helps keep them from making mistakes.

Splash!

People need to measure length carefully.

If a bridge is not long enough, people may fall in the water!

Did You Know?

Long ago, people used their feet to measure distance. People's feet were all different sizes. This meant they got different measurements.

Ouch!

People need to measure *temperature* carefully.

If something is very hot, it can burn a person.

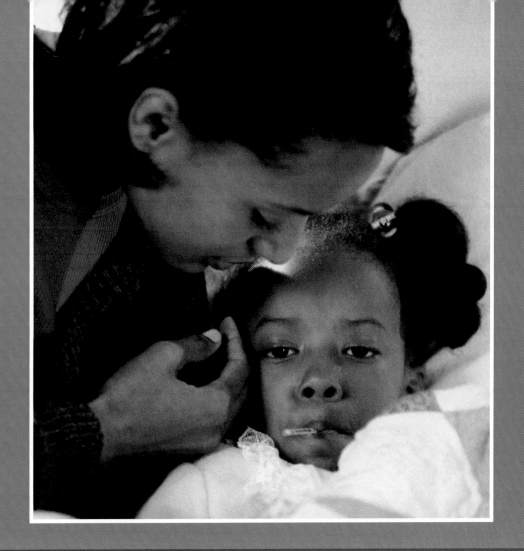

Did You Know?

People measure their temperature when they get sick. If their temperature is too high, they need to see a doctor.

Burned to a Crisp

People need to measure time carefully.

If toast cooks too long, it can burn. If a clock is wrong, a person could miss the bus.

Did You Know?

People can measure time by using years, months, days, hours, minutes, and seconds.

13

Bubbles Everywhere

People need to measure *volume* carefully.

If someone uses too much soap in the washing machine, it will spill bubbles all over the floor.

Did You Know?

It is important to measure volume correctly when cooking. Cookies made with a teaspoon of salt taste good. Cookies made with a tablespoon of salt taste bad.

Ticket Time

People need to measure speed carefully.

If a car is moving too fast it can be in an *accident.*

Did You Know?

Police officers use speed guns to measure how fast people are driving. If people go too fast, they can get a speeding ticket.

The Right Tool

People need to measure with the correct tool. A teaspoon can measure volume. Still, it would be silly to use a teaspoon to measure how much water is in a swimming pool.

Did You Know?

Sometimes measurements can be surprising. A pound of cotton is bigger than a pound of marbles. They weigh the same, but they have different volumes.

Fun Facts

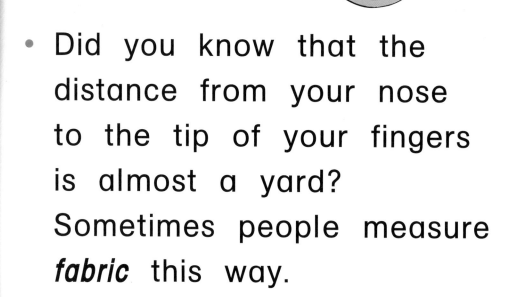

- A calendar measures time in days. A stopwatch measures time in **fractions** of a second.

- Did you know that the distance from your nose to the tip of your fingers is almost a yard? Sometimes people measure **fabric** this way.

- Horses are measured in hands. A hand is four inches (ten centimeters).

- Many foods have their weight printed on the packaging.

Glossary

accident–something that was not supposed to happen

fabric–cloth or material

fraction–a small part of something

measure–to find out the size or weight of something

temperature–how hot or cold something is

twice–two times

volume–the amount of space that something takes up

Learn More

Books

Koomen, Michele. *Size: Many Ways to Measure.* Mankato, Minn.: Bridgestone Books, 2001.

Pistoia, Sara. *Time.* Chanhassen, Minn.: Child's World, 2002.

Waters, Jennifer. *Measure It!* Minneapolis, Minn.: Compass Point Books, 2002.

Web Sites

Brain POP

www.brainpop.com/science/seeall.weml
(click on "measurement")

PBS Kids

http://pbskids.org/cyberchase/games.html
(try "Wacky Ruler" or "Can You Fill It?")

Index

distance, 9, 20

height, 6

length, 8

speed, 16, 17

temperature, 10, 11

time, 12, 13, 20

volume, 14, 15, 18, 19

weight, 19, 21

GR: H
Word Count: 178

From Janine Scott

I live in New Zealand and have two daughters. They love to read books that are full of fun facts and features. I hope you do, too!

24